Options for the Management of White Pine Blister Rust in the Rocky Mountain Region

United States
Department
of Agriculture

Forest Service

Rocky Mountain
Research Station

General Technical
Report RMRS-GTR-206

March 2008

Kelly S. Burns
Anna W. Schoettle
William R. Jacobi
Mary F. Mahalovich

I0454945

Burns, Kelly S.; Schoettle, Anna W.; Jacobi, William R.; Mahalovich, Mary F. 2008. **Options for the management of white pine blister rust in the Rocky Mountain Region.** Gen. Tech. Rep. RMRS-GTR-206. Fort Collins, CO: U.S. Department of Agriculture, Forest Service, Rocky Mountain Research Station. 26 p.

Abstract

This publication synthesizes current information on the biology, distribution, and management of white pine blister rust (WPBR) in the Rocky Mountain Region. In this Region, WPBR occurs within the range of Rocky Mountain bristlecone pine (*Pinus aristata*), limber pine (*P. flexilis*), and whitebark pine (*P. albicaulis*). This disease threatens white pine species and ecosystems in some of our most treasured public and private lands, including the wildland-urban interface, Wilderness Areas, and National Parks such as Rocky Mountain National Park and Great Sand Dunes National Park and Preserve. Long-term management strategies and management options for sustaining ecosystems and preserving high-value trees are presented. This information provides forest managers with knowledge and resources needed to detect WPBR, evaluate impacted stands, and develop management strategies that are applicable in the Rocky Mountain Region.

Keywords: white pine blister rust, five-needle pines, exotic pathogen, silviculture, restoration, disease management

Authors

Kelly S. Burns, Pathologist, USDA Forest Service, Rocky Mountain Region, Forest Health Management, Lakewood Service Center, Golden, CO

Anna W. Schoettle, Research Plant Ecophysiologist, USDA Forest Service, Rocky Mountain Research Station, Fort Collins, CO

William R. Jacobi, Professor, Colorado State University, Department of Bioagricultural Sciences and Pest Management, Fort Collins, CO

Mary F. Mahalovich, Geneticist, USDA Forest Service, Northern, Rocky Mountain, Southwestern, and Intermountain Regions, Moscow, ID

cover photos (clockwise beginning top left): A stem canker causes topkill in limber pine; close-up of rust blisters and spores; using a pole pruner to collect RM bristlecone pine cones; screening RM bristlecone pine for blister rust resistance; white pine regeneration following fire.

You may order additional copies of this publication by sending your mailing information in label form through one of the following media. Please specify the publication title and series number.

Fort Collins Service Center

Telephone	(970) 498-1392
FAX	(970) 498-1122
E-mail	rschneider@fs.fed.us
Web site	http://www.fs.fed.us/rm/publications
Mailing address	Publications Distribution
	Rocky Mountain Research Station
	240 West Prospect Road
	Fort Collins, CO 80526

Rocky Mountain Research Station
Natural Resources Research Center
2150 Centre Avenue, Bldg. A
Fort Collins, Colorado 80526

Contents

Introduction

White pine blister rust (WPBR) is an exotic, invasive fungal disease of white, stone, and foxtail pines (also referred to as white pines or five-needle pines) in the genus *Pinus* and subgenus *Strobus* (Price and others 1998). The disease, which is native to Asia, was accidentally introduced separately into eastern and western North America at the beginning of the 20th century. In the West, WPBR was introduced on infected eastern white pine (*Pinus strobus*) nursery stock shipped to Vancouver, B.C., from France in 1910. Since then, the disease has spread into the distributions of most western white pines. Although all of the North American white pine species are susceptible to WPBR (Bingham 1972, Hoff and others 1980), it was once thought that the remote, dry habitats occupied by the noncommercial, high elevation white pines would not support rust establishment. Unfortunately, WPBR can now be found in many of these areas.

Cronartium ribicola, the fungus that causes WPBR, requires an alternate host—currants and gooseberries in the genus *Ribes* and possibly species of *Pedicularis* and *Castilleja* (McDonald and others 2006, Zambino and others 2007)—to complete its life cycle. WPBR infects *Ribes* seasonally, causing minimal damage such as leaf spots and premature defoliation. The infections are shed each year with leaf abscission. The disease is perennial on infected pines, causing cankers that usually lead to mortality. WPBR has killed millions of acres of trees resulting in dramatic changes in successional pathways and ecosystem functions, and the disease continues to spread and intensify wherever five-needle pines occur despite control efforts.

Management strategies have been developed for the commercial white pine species, but these strategies have not been tested on the high elevation, noncommercial species. The Rocky Mountain Region is in a unique position in that a large portion of our susceptible white pine distribution is currently not yet impacted by blister rust. It may be possible to implement proactive management strategies in threatened areas that may prevent or mitigate severe impacts in the future. The objective of this publication is to provide land managers with the knowledge and tools necessary to identify WPBR, evaluate impacted stands, and develop appropriate management strategies for preserving high-value trees, restoring impacted stands, and sustaining white pine ecosystems in the Rocky Mountain Region.

Hosts

White pines are well distributed within the forested areas of the Rocky Mountain Region, particularly in Colorado and Wyoming (fig. 1). Pine hosts include whitebark pine (*Pinus albicaulis*), limber pine (*P. flexilis*), Rocky Mountain bristlecone pine (*P. aristata*), and southwestern white pine (*P. strobiformis*). The only susceptible species that remains uninfected in the Rocky Mountain Region is southwestern white pine. However, southwestern white pine is infected throughout much of its range in New Mexico (Conklin 2004).

Whitebark pine

The southeastern portion of the distribution of whitebark pine is in the Rocky Mountain Region. Blister rust-infected whitebark pines were first observed in the Coast Range of British Columbia in 1926 and in the northern Rocky Mountains in 1938 (Childs and others 1938). Mortality caused by the disease is greatest in whitebark pine stands of the northern Rockies where infection levels are variable but levels of over 70 percent are common (Kendall and Keane 2001; Schwandt 2006). Recent surveys estimate the incidence in the more recently infected Greater Yellowstone Ecosystem is approximately 25 percent (Greater Yellowstone Whitebark Pine Monitoring Working Group 2006). The species is early seral in the subalpine forests and can define upper treeline in some areas. Whitebark pine is successively replaced by subalpine fir (*Abies lasiocarpa*) in the absence of stand-replacing fire. The seeds of whitebark pine are large and wingless and enclosed in a cone that does not open upon ripening. Clark's nutcrackers (*Nucifraga columbiana*) extract the seeds and serve as the primary dispersal mechanism. A number of other scatter-hoarding birds and small mammals contribute slightly to seed dispersal, such as red squirrels (*Tamiasciurus hudsonicus*) and grizzly bears (*Ursus arctos horribilis*), which consume white pine seeds as an important part of their diet.

Limber pine

Limber pine is widely distributed in the western United States. The southern portion of its distribution in the Rockies is within the Rocky Mountain Region. Infected limber pines were first observed in the Rocky Mountains in the 1940s (Krebill 1964) and within the Rocky Mountain Region in the 1960s (Brown 1978). In the northern Rocky Mountains, limber pine generally occurs at lower elevations. In the Rocky Mountain

White pine species

- RM bristlecone pine
- Limber pine
- Whitebark pine

0 50 100 200 Miles

N

Figure 1. Distribution of susceptible white pine species in the Rocky Mountain Region based on USGS Gap Analysis Program (GAP) vegetation data. The distribution of southwestern white pine overlaps with that of limber pine in southwest Colorado. Because of its limited distribution, southwestern white pine is not depicted in the GAP dataset.

Region, limber pine has a very wide elevational range, from the grassland-forest ecotone at 5,250 ft to the subalpine-alpine ecotone at 11,482 ft and everywhere in between (Schoettle and Rochelle 2000). Dave's Draw Research Natural Area on the Pawnee National Grassland contains one of the unique peripheral populations of limber pine. Limber pine is a common species along the Colorado Front Range and is widely distributed in Rocky Mountain National Park. Like whitebark pine, the seeds are wingless (or nearly wingless) and rely on the Clark's nutcracker for dispersal. In contrast to whitebark pine, limber pine cones open upon seed maturity. Its seeds also provide food for squirrels and may therefore affect Canada lynx (*Lynx Canadensis*) prey populations. Limber pine tends to be one of the first species established after fire on dry

sites and can facilitate the establishment of other species that can eventually replace it on more mesic sites. This species can tolerate very harsh, exposed sites and is very long-lived (greater than 1,000 years old).

Rocky Mountain bristlecone pine

Almost the entire distribution of RM bristlecone pine is within the Rocky Mountain Region, with a small portion of its distribution extending into northern New Mexico and an isolated population in central Arizona. This species was distinguished from Great Basin bristlecone pine (*Pinus longaeva*) in 1970 (Bailey 1970). RM bristlecone, like Great Basin bristlecone, can be very long-lived, reaching life spans of over 2,600 years old. *P. aristata* has broad distribution in central Colorado and is the main attraction at the

Table 1—*Ribes* species that grow in association with white pine populations in the Rocky Mountain Region and their potential for contributing to the spread of white pine blister rust (Kearns 2005; Van Arsdel and Geils 2004).

Species[a]	Common name	Potential for contributing to disease spread
Ribes cereum	wax currant	usually insignificant but unknown
R. inerme	whitestem gooseberry	moderate or variable
R. lacustre	prickly currant	moderate or variable
R. montigenum	gooseberry currant	moderate or variable
R. laxiflorum	trailing black currant	moderate or variable
R. hudsonianum	northern black currant	high
R. viscosissimum	sticky currant	moderate or variable

[a] Species listed in order of abundance based on Kearns (2005).

Mount Goliath Research Natural Area on the Arapaho National Forest and Windy Ridge Natural Area on the Pike National Forest. An interpretive center was recently added at the entrance to the Research Natural Area to further highlight this unique species for the estimated 100,000 annual visitors. RM bristlecone pine is primarily a subalpine species and commonly defines upper treeline; however, it can also grow in and amongst ponderosa pine (*P. ponderosa*) and piñon pine (*P. edulis*). Like limber pine, it forms long-lived stands on dry exposed slopes and ridges and regenerates well after fire. This species has winged seeds that are wind-dispersed but are also dispersed by nutcrackers and other corvids.

Southwestern white pine

The northern-most portion of the distribution of southwestern white pine is within the Rocky Mountain Region in southwest Colorado. WPBR has not been observed on southwestern white pine in Colorado to date. It is thought that limber pine and southwestern white pine may hybridize, which could complicate distribution and range information. Like limber and whitebark pine, southwestern white pine in Colorado has wingless or near-wingless seeds, but the seed dispersal mechanisms are not fully understood.

Ribes species

Many species of *Ribes* occur in the Rocky Mountain Region and they vary both in their susceptibility to blister rust and capacity to support inoculum (see table 1) (Kearns 2005; Van Arsdel and Geils 2004). Distribution surveys indicate that one or more susceptible *Ribes* species occur in all white pine habitats and at all elevations in the region (Kearns 2005). Our most common species, *Ribes cereum*, occurs at lower elevations and on drier sites and is reported to be an insignificant host (Van Arsdel and Geils 2004). However, infected *R. cereum* leaves were collected from a heavily infected bush located on Pole Mountain, Wyoming,

in 2004 and *Cronartium ribicola* infection was confirmed using DNA analysis (D.R. Vogler, personal communication). This suggests that *R. cereum* may have a larger role in disease spread and intensification in the Rocky Mountain Region than was previously thought.

Other alternate hosts

Recently, researchers observed naturally occurring *C. ribicola* infections on sickletop lousewort (*Pedicularis racemosa*), bracted lousewort (*P. bracteosa*), and common red paintbrush (*Castilleja miniata*), suggesting that plants other than *Ribes* may also serve as alternate hosts (McDonald and others 2006; Zambino and others 2007). This new discovery could affect our understanding of WPBR epidemiology in some ecosystems.

Current Distribution of White Pine Blister Rust in the Rocky Mountain Region and Surrounding Areas

WPBR was first discovered on *Ribes* in Wyoming in Yellowstone National Park in 1944 (USDA Forest Service 1950), but infected pines were not discovered in that area until 1950 (USDA Forest Service 1951). The disease front has slowly progressed east and south since then. Infected pines were reported on the Shoshone National Forest in 1966 (Brown 1967), the Bighorn National Forest in 1959 (USDA Forest Service 1959; Brown 1967), and Laramie Peak, Medicine Bow National Forest, in 1969 (Brown 1978). An examination of limber pine on Pole Mountain in the early 1980s revealed light infection levels (B.W. Geils, personal communication). Kearns (2007) recently completed the most comprehensive survey of central and south-central Wyoming and for the first time, reported the disease in the Medicine Bow and Sierra Madre Mountains (Kearns and Burns 2005). Incidence of WPBR was greatest in northern Wyoming and in areas where the disease has been present for decades. Currently, the incidence of WPBR is low in the Medicine Bow and Sierra Madre Mountains.

WPBR was discovered on limber pine in North Dakota (Draper and Walla 1993) and South Dakota (Lundquist and others 1992) in 1992. In 1990, the disease was discovered on southwestern white pine in the Sacramento Mountains of southern New Mexico on the Lincoln National Forest (Hawksworth 1990). Subsequent surveys in New Mexico identified the disease in several other locations farther north, including the White Mountains, Mescalero Apache Reservation, Capitan Mountains, and Gallinas Peak (Conklin 2004; Geils and others 1999). In 2005, WPBR was discovered on southwestern white pine in western New Mexico only 3 miles from the Arizona border. In 2006, the disease was discovered in northern New Mexico in the Jemez Mountains (D.A. Conklin, personal

communication). The disease has never been reported in Arizona.

WPBR has been present on National Forests in Idaho since the 1960s (Brown and Graham 1969; Krebill 1964), but was only recently discovered in western and northeastern Nevada (Smith and others 2000, Vogler and Charlet 2004). Infected *Ribes inerme* leaves were observed in Carbon County, Utah, in 2005 (B.W. Geils and D.R. Vogler, personal communication), but the disease has never been reported on pine hosts in that state.

WPBR was discovered in Colorado in 1998 on limber pine in the Roosevelt National Forest in the north-central part of the state just below the Colorado-Wyoming border (Johnson and Jacobi 2000). These new infections were likely the result of southward spread from Wyoming where the disease has been present for decades (Brown 1978). Other parts of

Figure 2. Current distribution of white pine blister rust in the Rocky Mountain Region.

USDA Forest Service RMRS-GTR-206. 2008.

Colorado had not been surveyed extensively until 2002 when a study to monitor blister rust spread and establishment was initiated in the central and southern Rocky Mountains. Surprisingly, field crews discovered infected trees on the San Isabel National Forest in the Sangre de Cristo and Wet Mountains of southern Colorado. Infections in southern Colorado were found primarily on limber pine, but infected Rocky Mountain bristlecone pines were also observed for the first time in their native range (Blodgett and Sullivan 2004a, b). In 2005, WPBR was discovered 4.5 miles southeast of Estes Park, Colorado (R. Beam and J. Klutsch, personal communication), and in 2006, the disease was discovered 4 miles north of Nederland, Colorado (J.T. Hoffman, personal communication). Great Basin bristlecone pine (*Pinus longaeva*) and Mexican white pine (*Pinus ayacahuite*) are the only native five-needle pines that remain uninfected in North America. The current distribution of WPBR in the Rocky Mountain Region is displayed in figure 2.

Disease Cycle

Cronartium ribicola has a complex life cycle involving five different spore stages (fig. 3)—two that occur on pines (pycniospore, aeciospore) and three that occur on *Ribes* leaves (urediniospore, teliospore, basidiospore). The aeciospore, urediniospore, and basidiospore stages are the most important spore stages in terms of disease spread.

WPBR cannot spread from pine to pine but is transmitted to pines from basidiospores produced on infected *Ribes* leaves. Basidiospores are small, fragile, and short-lived and primarily disperse short distances (usually less than 1,000 feet, but possibly up to several miles). Pines are infected through needle stomata in the late summer and early fall. Germination and infection occur when nighttime temperatures stay cool (below 68°F), free moisture is available on the needle surface, and relative humidity is very high for at least 2 consecutive days (Van Arsdel and others 2005). Following

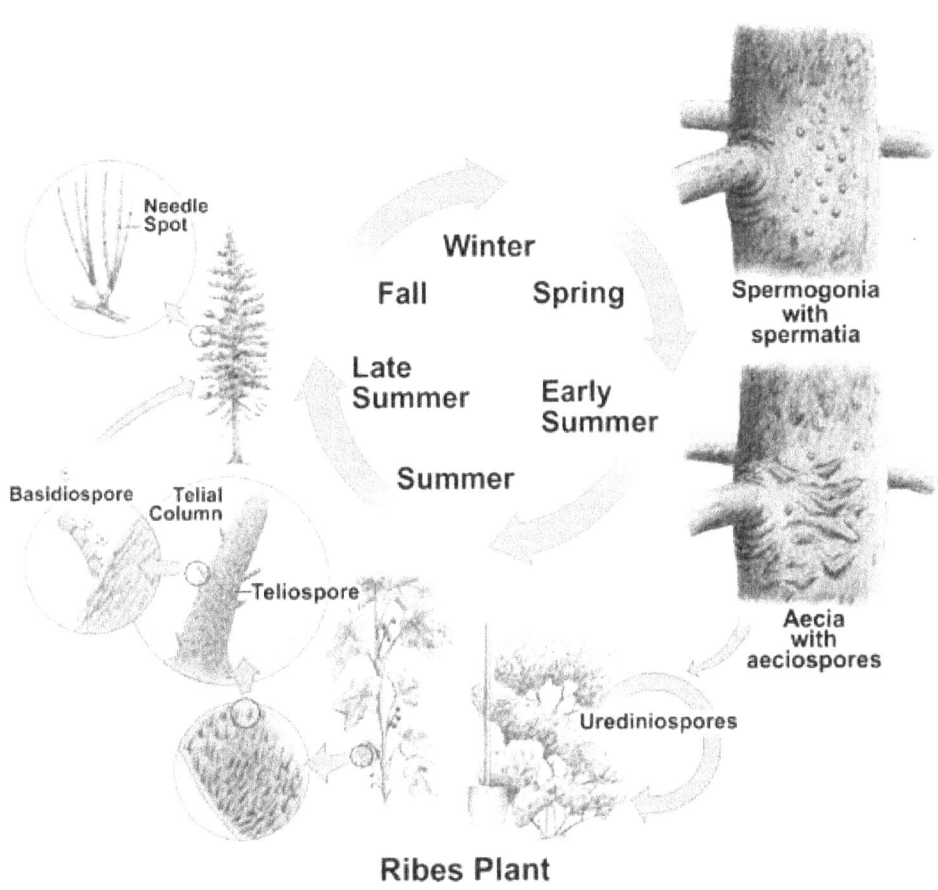

Figure 3. White pine blister rust disease cycle.

infection, the fungus grows down the needle and into the bark where a canker forms. The first spores to appear on the pine in the summer or early fall are haploid pycniospores (spermatia) produced in a nectar-like secretion within spore structures called pycnia (spermogonia) near the canker margin. These spores are not infectious but are involved in fertilization. Insects, attracted to the sweet liquid, carry pycniospores to other nearby pycnia where they may fuse with and fertilize receptive hyphae, subsequently producing dikaryotic mycelium. The following year, aeciospores are produced in the fertilized portion of the canker and haploid mycelium continues to spread into healthy tissue producing pycnia and pyniospores annually. Blisters (aecia) packed with bright orange aeciospores erupt though the cankered bark in spring and early summer. Aeciospores are hardy, thick-walled spores that can travel long distances (potentially hundreds of miles) in the wind to infect susceptible *Ribes* hosts.

Orange urediniospores are produced in pustules (uredinia) on the underside of infected *Ribes* leaves throughout the summer when climatic conditions are favorable (temperatures between 57.2 and 68°F) (Van Arsdel and others 2005). These spores are relatively fragile and usually travel very short distances to re-infect *Ribes* leaves. Thus, they increase inoculum levels, but they cannot infect pines. In the fall, brown hair-like columns (telia) of teliospores form on infected *Ribes* leaves. Teliospores germinate to form basidiospores that later infect pines, completing the cycle.

Generally, cool temperatures and high relative humidity favor disease spread and intensification. The incidence of pine infection may increase substantially during years when optimum environmental conditions coincide with spore production, dissemination, germination, and infection. These are often referred to as "wave years." In the Rocky Mountain Region, the disease is more prevalent in valley bottoms and at lower elevations, presumably where these conditions occur more frequently (Burns 2006; Kearns 2007).

Impacts of White Pine Blister Rust

Tree Damage

North American white pines did not evolve with *Cronartium ribicola* and therefore have little resistance to the pathogen, and there are few natural enemies to regulate spread and intensification of the disease. Once a canker forms on a tree, it will usually continue to expand killing bark tissues as it grows.

Eventually, the branch or stem is girdled and distal portions of the tree die. Twig beetles, wood borers, and rodents are commonly found contributing to the death of cankered branches. Ultimately, the entire tree may be killed depending on the location and number of cankers. Trees weakened by blister rust may become susceptible to other damaging agents such as bark beetles. WPBR may significantly impact reproductive potential by weakening and ultimately killing cone-bearing branches. It affects trees of all ages and sizes and could potentially eliminate white pines from certain ecosystems and landscapes. Small trees are especially susceptible because most infections occur close to the main stem girdling the tree.

Stem cankers usually kill the portion of the tree above the canker causing topkill, while branch cankers kill the distal portion of the branch. Because *C. ribicola* is an obligate parasite and requires living tissue to persist, it will die if the branch dies before the fungus reaches the main stem. Generally, the probability of branch infections reaching the bole declines with distance, and branch infections more than 24 inches from the trunk will usually kill the branch before reaching the main stem (Childs and Kimmey 1938; Hunt 1982). Branch infections that reach the main stem can cause topkill and mortality. In the Rocky Mountain Region, it is not unusual for mortality to result without a stem infection when numerous branch infections occur throughout the crown.

Ecological Consequences

White pines serve many important ecological functions. They provide food for wildlife, stabilize slopes, help regulate snow and runoff, and maintain cover on harsh, rugged sites where little else can grow (Schoettle 2004a). They are some of the oldest and largest pines in the Rocky Mountain Region and are especially valued because of their unique cultural and ecological characteristics.

WPBR may greatly alter or devastate ecosystems. For example, in heavily impacted areas, reduced post-fire reforestation and reduced sustainability of bird and wildlife species may result. On sites where limber pine is the only tree species present and mortality is high, hydrologic changes and slope instability could occur. In the drier areas of the region, post-fire forest recovery is likely to be slowed by the WPBR-impaired regeneration capacity of limber and bristlecone pines. See the **No Intervention** section for further discussion of ecological impacts of WPBR.

Detection and Evaluation

Symptoms, Signs, and Field Identification

Bright red, recently killed "flagged branches" are the most obvious symptom of WPBR from a distance; however, other agents, such as dwarf mistletoe and twig beetles, can also cause flagging. The best time to positively identify infected trees in the field is when aecia are most visible. Generally, this occurs in May or early June depending on local weather conditions. The first conspicuous symptom on pine is a small, diamond-shaped swelling with an orange margin where the fungus is most active (fig. 4). Pycnia (spermogonia) form, usually in summer or early fall, within the canker the following year—they are small, dark brown, and blister-like. Pycnia rupture, oozing pycniospores (spermatia) that appear as orange liquid droplets (fig. 5). Aecia form the next year in the same tissue as pycnia. Aecia appear as white sacs full of bright

Figure 4. The advancing edge of the canker is bright orange and rodent-feeding is common.

Figure 5. Pycniospores (spermatia) appear as orange liquid droplets.

Figure 6. Blisters (aecia) filled with bright orange spores (aeciospores) rupture through the bark in the spring.

orange aeciospores easily visible as they rupture in the spring and early summer (fig. 6). After aeciospores are released, the cankered bark becomes roughened, dark, and resinous as it dies while the fungus continues to expand into the healthy tissue surrounding the canker. The branch or stem is eventually girdled and killed. It is common for rodents to gnaw off the cankered bark (fig. 4). Rodent gnawing may indicate rust or mistletoe infections.

Field identification of WPBR on *Ribes* can be confusing because the distribution of our native piñon blister rust (*Cronartium occidentale*) overlaps with that of *C. ribicola* throughout Colorado, and both rusts use *Ribes* species as alternate hosts. The two fungi look very similar macroscopically, but can be differentiated in the field when carefully examined (Van Arsdel and Geils 2004). Symptoms of WPBR on *Ribes* are most obvious in the fall when telial columns form on the undersurface of leaves. Telia are orange-brown, sparsely distributed, and hair-like. Uredinia form earlier in the summer and appear as yellow-orange pustules scattered over the undersurface of the leaf. In the near future, Colorado State University's Plant Disease Clinic will be able to perform DNA analysis on infected *Ribes* leaves to distinguish between the various rust species.

Surveys and Monitoring

Surveying white pine stands for blister rust and monitoring impacts over time are critical for successful management. Surveying is done to detect new infestations and determine the extent and distribution of the disease. Changes in the incidence and severity of the disease and resulting ecological impacts over time can be documented by monitoring permanent plots. Information obtained through surveying and monitoring will allow managers to plan and prioritize forest stands for proactive management and restoration.

Several protocols are available for surveying and monitoring whitebark pine and these may be transferable to other white pines in the Rocky Mountain Region. Standardized methods developed by the Whitebark Pine Ecosystem Foundation (WPEF) can be downloaded from its website: http://www.whitebarkfound.org (Tomback and others 2004). The Greater Yellowstone Whitebark Pine Monitoring Working Group (GYWPMWG) has also developed methods for monitoring the long-term health of Greater Yellowstone Ecosystem whitebark pine populations. The group uses a more conservative approach to positively identifying WPBR-caused cankers than does the WPEF. Its approach requires that at least three ancillary indicators (flagging, rodent chewing, oozing sap, roughened bark, and swelling) are present when aecia are not visible (GYWPMWG 2006). Additionally, specific survey methods were developed for the whitebark pine genetic restoration program to identify plus trees, develop seed transfer guidelines, and later, develop a selective breeding program. This protocol requires more observations (100 trees per plot are recommended) than the WPEF or GYWPMWG methods and is summarized in the Identifying Plus Trees section (Mahalovich and Dickerson 2004).

Managers are strongly encouraged to consult with Forest Health personnel to develop appropriate methods for surveying and monitoring white pine stands that are consistent with the USDA Forest Service, Natural Resource Information System, Field Sampled Vegetation (FSVeg).

Hazard and Risk Rating

Risk rating is used to predict the likelihood of WPBR establishment on a site, while hazard rating is used to predict the amount of tree damage that can be expected as a result of the disease. Both hazard and risk rating may be useful tools for WPBR management in the Rocky Mountain Region.

Hazard rating

The incidence and severity of blister rust is strongly influenced by host genetics, the proximity and abundance of hosts, and microclimate (Geils and others 1999). Knowledge of rust epidemiology, combined with information on forest and climatic conditions, can be used to model hazard to help determine the expected extent and impact of the disease and to guide management. Hazard can be quantified several different ways, such as the proportion of infected trees, percent mortality, or the number and severity of cankers. By delineating rust hazard zones, managers can focus white pine management in those areas where successful management is more likely and prepare for restoration in areas predicted to be heavily impacted. Hazard rating has been used in the Lake States (Katovich and others 2004), British Columbia (Hunt 1983), eastern United States (Charlton 1963), and Northern Region (Hagle and others 1989).

Development of a WPBR hazard model for Colorado has been attempted, but the model could not predict hazard across such a vast geographic area with a high degree of accuracy (Kearns 2005). The hazard model predicts that disease incidence will be higher in areas with increased years of exposure to the pathogen, longer frost-free periods and warmer nighttime temperatures in September, and higher levels of precipitation in July. In a survey of northern Colorado and Wyoming, Kearns (2005) found that disease incidence was significantly correlated with elevation and slope position, with higher disease incidences at lower elevations and slope positions. Similarly, Burns (2006) found a significant negative relationship between both disease presence and incidence and elevation in a survey of the Sangre de Cristo and Wet Mountains of southern Colorado. These relationships likely reflect more conducive climatic conditions at lower elevations in Colorado and Wyoming. However, in New Mexico, disease incidence increases with elevation (Geils and others 1999), suggesting that it is important to base hazard on climatic conditions and not elevation alone.

Risk rating

The potential distribution (risk) of WPBR for white pines in Colorado was modeled using PRISM climate data (Daly and others 2002) and data from 329 limber pine plots and 754 *Ribes* plots installed throughout Wyoming and Colorado (Kearns 2005). *Ribes* density, stream density, and the number of potential infection episodes were major predictors of potential disease distribution. However, when PRISM climate data were added to the model, the following were selected as significant variables for predicting the presence or absence of rust in Colorado: (1) May relative humidity, (2) May minimum temperature, (3) May precipitation, and (4) August minimum temperature. Results suggest that approximately 50 percent of Colorado's white pine stands are at risk for blister rust establishment. Howell and others (2006) provide a summary of the WPBR model and how it can be applied on a local level.

Management Options

Despite efforts to control WPBR, the disease continues to spread and intensify. Control strategies have been developed for western white pine, sugar pine, and eastern white pine, but these strategies have not been tested on the white pines of the Rocky Mountain Region and they may not be applicable. Because whitebark pine is rapidly declining throughout much of its range, efforts are underway to promote whitebark pine restoration and conservation. Schwandt (2006) outlined whitebark pine restoration strategies and developed a manager's guide to help select the best management option under various stand conditions and circumstances. Restoration strategies for whitebark pine may be appropriate for other high elevation species. The Rocky Mountain Region is unique in that much of our susceptible white pine distribution is not yet impacted by WPBR and we may be able to prevent a catastrophe by implementing proactive management options. An evaluation of proactive management options to mitigate impacts before ecosystems are impaired can be found in Schoettle and Sniezko (2007).

The most sustainable, long-term solution may be to increase the frequency of rust resistance across the landscape (Samman and others 2003; Schoettle and Sniezko 2007; Schwandt 2006). In the short-term, management strategies such as pruning and *Ribes* removal to decrease inoculum potential may be used to reduce infections and prolong the life of existing trees, but these strategies will not increase resistance and sustainability over time and space. Specific management strategies and how they may be adapted to the Rocky Mountain Region are discussed in the following sections. WPBR management strategies have not been tested in the Rocky Mountain Region, and therefore any site-specific treatments will be experimental. Selection of a treatment option will depend on many factors, such as the level of current impacts, rust hazard or risk, frequency of resistance in the white pine population, site and stand conditions, and accessibility. The region is currently assessing the levels of rust resistance in our pine hosts. Managers are strongly encouraged to work closely with a forest health specialist when developing and implementing treatments.

No Intervention

The impacts of WPBR on high elevation forests of the northern Rockies demonstrates the ecological consequences of no intervention. These whitebark and limber pine forests have been challenged by WPBR for over 50 years and the impacts have been extensive with far-reaching effects on ecosystem function and biodiversity (Tomback and Kendell 2001). With no intervention to alter the trajectory of interaction between WPBR and white pines in the Rocky Mountain Region, WPBR can be expected to continue impacting ecosystem function as it spreads through the remaining white pine populations. Early stages of infection directly impact seed production and wildlife species that depend on white pine seeds. Reduced white pine regeneration capacity affects forest recovery after disturbances (especially fire), slows succession, and influences the distribution of other species due to the lack of facilitation (Schoettle 2004a). Increased tree mortality results in changes in forest structure, which in turn, influences snow capture, watershed hydrology, community diversity, and wildlife habitat and the sustainability of the forest type on the site. Seedlings and saplings are especially susceptible and are often killed or severely damaged. On sites where five-needle pines

are the only tree species present, high mortality may cause the sites to transition to treeless areas causing hydrologic changes and slope instability. The effect of WPBR-caused tree mortality on the fire ecology of these harsh sites is not known.

Strategies for Preserving Trees on High-value Sites

Ribes removal

Historically, blister rust control focused on eradicating *Ribes* bushes growing in and around white pine stands because the basidiospores that are transmitted from *Ribes* to pine are short-lived and usually only able to disperse short distances (see the **Disease Cycle** section). A *Ribes* eradication program was initiated in 1915 and became a massive national effort to save commercially valuable white pines. In the Rocky Mountain Region, *Ribes* eradication was attempted at several locations between the years of 1930 and 1964 prior to the arrival of WPBR. This included areas on the Shoshone, Medicine Bow, and Pike National Forests and Rocky Mountain National Park.

Ribes eradication proved to be effective in various isolated locations, primarily in the eastern United States (Martin 1944; Ostrofsky and others 1988), but the program had limited success in the west due the abundance, distribution, and hardiness of hosts, the rugged and inaccessible terrain, and possibly, the more open forest ecosystems. The effectiveness of *Ribes* removal has not been thoroughly evaluated in the Rocky Mountain Region, but severe infection levels have been observed in areas with as little as one *Ribes* bush per acre. The role of *Ribes* in disease spread and intensification in the west may be very complicated and is poorly understood (Newcomb 2003).

Complete eradication of *Ribes* is not practical or desirable because many species of wildlife use *Ribes* and plants are widely distributed and difficult to remove completely. *Ribes* removal may be appropriate in certain high-value areas (for example, campgrounds) where all plants within 0.6 miles (1 km) of the area to be protected can be easily located and completely removed. However, removal of *Ribes* bushes would have little impact on the incidence of WPBR if other alternate hosts are involved (McDonald and others 2006; Zambino and others 2007) or if long-distance movement of basidiospores is suspected. *Ribes* removal supplemented with preventive and/or sanitation pruning (see below) may slow disease spread and reduce mortality in certain high-value areas. This strategy may not completely eliminate new infections,

Table 2—General guidelines for timing fungicide applications in the Rocky Mountain Region.

Host	Infection		
	Aeciospore	Urediniospore	Basidiospore
Ribes	50 percent leaf expansion and then for 6 weeks	June 1–July 30	Not applicable
Pines	Not applicable	Not applicable	July 1–Sept 15

but could reduce the impacts of the disease on the existing trees to a manageable level.

Although *Ribes* plants can tolerate partial shade, they grow best in full sunlight. Therefore, silvicultural treatments that open up the canopy, such as thinning and partial cutting, may encourage *Ribes*. The effects of fire on *Ribes* vary substantially by species. Generally, fire will kill *Ribes* bushes in the short-term. However, *Ribes* plants may be favored by fire over time because they are able to regenerate by sprouting and from long-lived seed stored in the soil that germinates in response to scarification (Carey 1995; Marshall 1995a, b). In central Colorado, the density of *Ribes* bushes can more than double after wildfire in stands formerly dominated by RM bristlecone pine (Schoettle and others 2003). The species most commonly found on these sites was *R. cereum*, a relatively poor host, so the impact on rust hazard is unknown.

Ribes bushes can be removed by hand using a claw mattock. The root crown and about 4 inches of the root below the crown must be removed to ensure that resprouting does not occur. Improperly pulled and missed plants are common, so follow-up management is usually required. A more efficient option is to remove *Ribes* bushes with herbicides (Offord and others 1958). Spot and broadcast spraying have both been used successfully. The effectiveness of chemical control varies with the type and amount of chemical used, physiological conditions of *Ribes*, climatic conditions, site factors, and method of application. Assistance of a qualified pesticide specialist is required.

Chemical controls of white pine blister rust

Chemical controls of WPBR are not practical in forest situations and will not contribute to long-term ecosystem sustainability. However, the use of fungicides in urban, nursery, and high-value sites such as campgrounds may be an effective management technique. Fungicides can be applied to *Ribes* or pines during the growing season to prevent WPBR infection. Preventing infection on the pine host is the preferred action since pines can be killed by the fungus, but protection of *Ribes* from defoliation by the rust may be

beneficial in certain circumstances. Fungicides must be applied prior to the infection episode(s) and be present on leaves or needles before spores are deposited. Table 2 provides general guidelines for timing fungicide application in the Rocky Mountain Region.

Fungicides in the ethylenebisdithiocarbamate (EBDC) class of compounds are active against rust fungi. Trade names include Penncozeb, Dithane, and Manx[1]. Systemic chemicals in the triazole class, such as Bayleton (Triadimefon), are potentially effective for a longer period. Triadimefon has been shown to effectively protect seedlings from WPBR infection (Berube 1996; Johnson and others 1992). Slow-release fertilizer plugs containing triadimefon are currently being tested for their effectiveness at preventing infection (Hoff and others 2001).

Protective fungicides applied according to label instructions should protect plants for 7 to 20 days depending on chemical and environmental conditions. Complete coverage of leaf and needle surfaces is critical, so application to large pines is not advised. Repeated applications may be required to protect pines during the infection period, which runs from approximately July 1 to the first frost.

State rules and regulations and special pesticide use allowances may vary from state to state. The State Department of Agriculture should be contacted for the rules, regulations, and applicable allowances in your state and locality.

In Colorado, the Colorado Environmental Pesticide Education Program website has the latest update on registered chemicals: http://www.colostate.edu/Depts/SoilCrop/extension/CEPEP/labels.htm.

---

[1] The information herein is supplied with the understanding that no discrimination is intended and that listing of commercial products, necessary to this guide, implies no endorsement by the authors or the USDA Forest Service. Pesticides must be applied legally complying with all label directions and precautions on the pesticide container and any supplemental labeling and rules of state and federal pesticide regulatory agencies.

Pruning

Pruning can be used to prolong the life of existing trees. It is not an effective long-term management strategy for increasing ecosystem resiliency because the progeny of pruned trees may still be susceptible to blister rust. Pruning of lower branches may be used as a preventive treatment. Sanitation pruning (also referred to as pathological pruning) of cankered branches is used to remove the infection before it reaches the main stem. A combination of both strategies may be most effective for protecting and preserving trees on a site.

Pruning is time consuming and expensive and thus best suited to high-value areas such as campgrounds, administrative sites, or areas where white pines are extremely important or the only species present.

Preventive pruning (crown raising)—Most lethal infections on western white pine, eastern white pine, and sugar pine occur in the lower one-third of the tree (Hungerford and others 1982; Hunt 1982; Lehrer 1982; Stillinger 1947) where environmental conditions are more favorable for infection (Van Arsdel 1961). These infections usually occur when trees are small and a large proportion of their foliage is close to the main stem. Crown raising or preventive pruning has been used successfully in these species when initiated at an early age. This type of pruning promotes disease escape by reducing the target for spores (Hagle and Grasham 1988; Hunt 1982; Lehrer 1982). Unfortunately, observations of infected limber, RM bristlecone, and southwestern white pine indicate that infections occur throughout the crown and are not concentrated near the ground (A. Crump and others, in preparation; Conklin 2004; Kearns 2005). Because of this, the efficacy of this strategy in the Rocky Mountain Region is questionable. However, infections in the upper crown may kill branches and tree tops, but not whole trees, so pruning lower branches may still protect trees from lethal infections.

General guidelines for conventional pruning are available online:

http://www.na.fs.fed.us/spfo/pubs/howtos/ht_prune/htprune.pdf

Specific guidelines for preventive pruning to manage WPBR include:

1. Initiate preventive pruning treatments when trees are 5 to 10 feet tall to reduce the probability of lethal infections (Schnepf and Schwandt 2006).

2. Remove small sprouts growing directly out of the bole (epicormic branches) since they can provide a direct infection court to the main stem. These branches and needles should be removed on the main stem and side branches within 24 inches of the main stem wherever possible. They can be pulled out by hand or with hand pruning shears.

Sanitation pruning (removing cankers) and excising—Selectively removing cankers, through sanitation pruning and excising (scribing a channel through the cambium to isolate the fungus), may reduce mortality of high-value trees by eliminating potentially lethal infections or those infections within 4 inches of the bole (Schnepf and Scwandt 2006). Colorado State University and the USDA Forest Service, Rocky Mountain Region have a study underway to evaluate the effectiveness of preventive pruning, sanitation pruning, and excising cankers for protecting trees and reducing mortality in limber and RM bristlecone pine. The effort required for preventive and/or sanitation pruning is on average 8 to 15 minutes per tree with a crew of two (A. Crump and others, in preparation). In the Rocky Mountain Region, limber pines are relatively short, so many cankers can be reached using hand tools from the ground. Hydraulic lifts may be a feasible alternative to ground-based tools for pruning tall trees on high-value sites.

Canker removal can be more time consuming and expensive than preventive pruning because a significant amount of time is required to identify and remove cankers throughout the crown and some cankers may be overlooked.

Specific guidelines for sanitation pruning and excising WPBR cankers include:

1. Treatments should occur when cankers are most visible. In the Rocky Mountain Region, this is usually during late May and early June, but depends on local weather conditions.

2. Cankers within 24 inches of the main stem need to be pruned (Hunt 1982).

3. Cankers within 4 inches of the main stem are potentially lethal and therefore need to be pruned and excised (Schnepf and Schwandt 2006).

4. Canker excision may be effective on trees if they have only one stem canker within 6 feet of the ground and if less than 50 percent of the bole circumference will be girdled following treatment (Hagle and others 1989; Schnepf and Schwandt 2006).

5. Cankers must be pruned or scribed at least 2 to 3 inches beyond the visible canker margin to ensure complete canker removal (Ehrhlich and Opie 1940; Hagle and others 1989). Lightly scrubbing a canker with water may help make the canker margins more visible.

6. Most potentially lethal infections occur in young trees because proportionally more of the susceptible foliage is close to the bole. Initiating pruning treatments early may prolong the life of trees (Hagle and others 1989; Hunt 1982; Schnepf and Schwandt 2006).

Thinning

Thinning white pine stands was believed to protect trees from blister rust because airflow between trees would increase, resulting in two beneficial effects: (1) a less favorable microclimate for infection to occur and (2) faster growing trees may be able to outgrow infections because branch cankers would die before reaching the main stem. However, studies in northern Idaho (Hungerford and others 1982; Schwandt and others 1994) found that thinning caused the incidence of lethal infections to increase, presumably because the treatment increased the amount of foliage exposed to inoculum and decreased the amount of self-pruning of lower branches. Thinning may also lead to increases in *Ribes*, which thrives in full sunlight. Similarly, Kearns (2007) found that the incidence of blister rust was higher on open-grown limber pines than on intermediate or overtopped trees. Thinning may be an appropriate management strategy under certain circumstances, especially if combined with pruning. In a study in northern Idaho, Schwandt and others (1994) found that western white pine stands that were thinned had increased mortality but survival and merchantability were greatly increased in stands that were thinned and pruned. Thinning may also be beneficial around potential plus trees to provide protection from fire and bark beetles, or it may be needed to facilitate regeneration.

Long-term Strategies

Identifying plus trees

It is not unusual to find one or more uninfected or lightly cankered trees in heavily infected stands, indicating that genetic resistance may be present. In general, the most resistant trees will remain alive and relatively unharmed longer than more susceptible trees. However, it is possible that uninfected trees are genetically susceptible to WPBR but "escape" infection for one reason or another. Therefore, it is advisable to test for genetic resistance through progeny testing.

Identifying plus (putatively resistant) trees should be a priority in severely infected areas and seed should be collected for restoration and resistance screening, particularly in areas threatened by mountain pine beetles (*Dendroctonus ponderosae*) (Schwandt 2006). Natural regeneration can be encouraged from plus trees and seed and pollen can be collected for gene conservation, resistance screening, and artificial regeneration.

As part of the genetic restoration program for whitebark pine, Mahalovich and Dickerson (2004) outline guidelines for selecting whitebark pine plus trees in moderately (50 to 90 percent infection) and severely (greater than 90 percent infection) infected stands. This protocol requires a blister rust survey on a representative sample of 100 trees to determine the average blister rust infection level for the stand. Candidate plus trees are then selected based on the stand average number of cankers per tree. For example, if the stand average (cankers/tree) is between 10 and 20, then candidate plus trees should be free of cankers. If the stand average is between 41 and 75, then plus trees should have no more than two cankers. Candidate plus trees do not need to be of perfect form and condition, but they should be free of other insects and diseases and be bearing at least 10 or more cones (Mahalovich and Hoff 2000). These guidelines were developed for whitebark pine but may be applicable to limber, southwestern white, and Rocky Mountain bristlecone pine. An assessment of operational guidelines for seed tree collections for limber pine in the Rocky Mountain Region is underway (STDP project R2-2006-02). Guidelines for cone and seed collections in whitebark pine are provided by Burr and others (2001) and Mahalovich (2007).

Establishing a Breeding Program

The most promising strategy for managing WPBR is to increase disease resistance (Samman and others 2003; Schoettle and Sniezko 2007; Schwandt 2006). The most elaborate approach would be a rust resistance breeding program involving several steps:

1. Seed is collected from putatively resistant trees in the forest.

2. Progeny are screened for resistance in the greenhouse.

3. Resistant progeny are established in a seed orchard.

4. Controlled crosses can be performed and seed can be supplied for restoration and reforestation (Mahalovich 2000).

Unfortunately, the high elevation white pines are slow to reach reproductive maturity (30 to 50 years in nature, but may be accelerated in a nursery setting) so this approach will require considerable time and sustained commitment. Interim resistant seed can be obtained by collecting cones from plus trees that showed above-average resistance to blister rust in the rust screening. Cone collections can be made from individual plus trees or the entire stand (seed production area) can be cultured for cone production. Additional resistance can be achieved through a selective breeding program. Researchers have recently identified major gene resistance in populations of southwestern white pine and limber pine (Kinloch and Dupper 1999), and levels of genetic resistance and resistance mechanisms in white pines of the Rocky Mountain Region are currently being analyzed in controlled inoculation studies. However, even when genetic resistance is found, there is the possibility that it could be overcome by more virulent races of the pathogen (McDonald and Hoff 2001). This is particularly true for resistance mechanisms that are controlled by a single gene.

Planting

Artificial regeneration may be necessary to restore and/or regenerate areas without an adequate natural seed supply or natural resistance (Hoff and others 2001). Seedlings should be grown from putatively resistant parent trees, preferably those from which resistance has been confirmed. White pine seedlings require bright sunlight, so cutting or prescribed burning may be necessary to open up the forest canopy. Planting resistant stock could also be advisable before or in the early stages of blister rust invasion in high hazard areas if resistance is identified. Supplementing natural resistance within a stand with artificial regeneration with resistant stock early in the invasion process will minimize the window of time when the reproductive potential of the stand is compromised by rust-caused topkill or tree mortality (Schoettle and Sniezko 2007). The resistant seedlings will be approaching seed-bearing maturity as the seed-bearing capacity of the mature overstory is being reduced. In whitebark pine, it is recommended that managers plant double the number of seedlings needed to meet management objectives to make up for the many seedlings that will be killed by WPBR and other factors. Additionally, seedlings should be at least 3 years old to ensure higher survival rates. Seedlings will need to be protected from the sun to avoid desiccation. Providing a microsite such as stumps, boulders, logs, or shade cloths during planting will promote survival and protect seedlings from animals (Mahalovich and others 2006). Planting strategies for restoration of whitebark pine are outlined by Mahalovich and others (2006) and should be transferable to other high elevation white pines.

Encouraging Natural Regeneration and Providing for Selection

Inclusion of silvicultural treatments, such as prescribed fire or a group selection regeneration method, in a long-term disease management strategy may be effective at increasing the frequency of naturally occurring rust resistance and promoting ecosystem tolerance to blister rust (Schoettle 2004b; Schoettle and Sniezko 2007). The treatments can be implemented before or after infestation.

The white pines of the Rocky Mountain Region regenerate most successfully following disturbances, such as fire or harvesting, that create openings and expose bare mineral soil. Research is currently underway to evaluate various silvicultural strategies for promoting natural regeneration including:

• Creating canopy openings to encourage regeneration.

• Preferentially retaining white pines during thinning and fuels treatments.

• Using prescribed fire and harvesting to:

 - Remove other tree species that compete with white pines for growing space.

 - Remove competing vegetation from around seedlings and saplings to promote their survival.

 - Prepare a seedbed for regeneration.

• Protecting potential seed trees from bark beetles using a preventive insecticide treatment or pheromones.

Before infestation

It may be possible to implement management strategies that will enhance white pine survival when challenged by blister rust (Schoettle and Sniezko 2007). Encouraging natural regeneration before WPBR has invaded a site will increase the likelihood of natural resistance in the future stand because selection pressure and susceptibility is strongest in young trees (Schoettle 2004b; Schoettle and Sniezko 2007). Creating a landscape of diverse age and size classes would facilitate rapid selection for resistance in the young trees while mature trees maintain ecosystem function and services (Schoettle and Sniezko 2007). Eventually, resistant seed will be produced when surviving trees reach reproductive age, furthering resilience of the population in the presence of the pathogen. This strategy will reduce the generation time of the long-lived pines and accelerate the evolution of resistance if the population becomes infected.

This proactive approach positions the ecosystem to use natural processes to provide resilience upon invasion and may be a cost effective option for many of the white pine forests in the southern portions of the Rocky Mountain Region that have not yet been infected or are in the early stages of infection. It may be especially suitable for ecosystems where minimal management has occurred historically and extensive restoration intervention is unlikely but the risk of ecological impacts is high. Assessment of the efficacy of this option for different species and geographic locations will be improved with knowledge of the frequency of heritable rust resistance in the native populations because the success of this approach relies on indigenous resistance within the population. If sufficient resistance is present (and early indications suggest it may be [Vogler and others 2006]) and sufficient regeneration is encouraged, this approach will accelerate the development of a forest with greater resistance that will be more capable of sustaining itself. Early outplanting of resistant stock (as discussed previously) will also contribute to increasing the frequency of rust resistance in the stand and may avert some ecological consequences of the invasion (Schoettle and Sniezko 2007).

After infestation

Encouraging regeneration after natural selection has acted on mature trees in the presence of WPBR has been proposed as a way to promote establishment of the progeny of the remaining, presumably resistant, mature trees (Hoff and others 1976). The white pines in the Rocky Mountain Region tend to regenerate best following disturbances and may respond well to a group selection regeneration method. However, under severe selection pressure (greater than 90 percent mortality) in these already open forests, it has been questioned whether enough seed is available to support natural regeneration (McKinney and Tomback 2007; Tomback and others 1995). In areas with high levels of mountain pine beetle activity, the number of mature trees may be further reduced and trees with rust resistance may be lost. Estimating the efficacy of this approach in the Rocky Mountain Region forests will be improved with further information on the regeneration ecology and levels of rust resistance in these species. In areas with high infection levels, artificial regeneration with rust-resistant stock may be the only option to increase rust-resistant individuals within the population and restore ecosystem function.

Other Management Considerations

Slowing the Spread of White Pine Blister Rust

Reducing the occurrence of infections at the leading edge of the infection front or in uninfected areas can slow the spread and intensification of WPBR.

- Learn to identify five-needle pines and currants and gooseberries and do not move plants from the forest. An educational pamphlet is available on the Rocky Mountain Region, Forest Health Management website (select "bulletin board"): http://www.fs.fed.us/r2/fhm/. Information is also available on the High Elevation White Pine website: http://www.fs.fed.us/rm/highelevationwhitepines/.
- Do not plant commercial nursery stock unless it is certified disease-free.
- Report blister rust sightings or suspicious trees to Forest Health Management.

Protection of Plus Trees

Fire

Fire will readily kill white pines since their bark is relatively thin (Howard 2002, 2004; Johnson 2001; Pavek 1993). Fire spread in white pine stands is often limited because of the open stand structure, scattered fuels, and sparse undergrowth. Thus, older trees may be able to withstand some stem scorch because their bark is thicker, especially at the base. Eliminating fuels surrounding plus trees will reduce the threat of fire damage.

Initially, fire may kill *Ribes* bushes, but in the long-term, *Ribes* is favored by fire because plants are able to regenerate from long-lived seed stored in the soil that germinates in response to scarification. *Ribes* may also sprout rapidly from root systems following mixed severity fires.

The USDA Forest Service Fire Effects Information System website (http://www.fs.fed.us/database/feis/) has detailed information on ecology and fire effects of the Rocky Mountain Region's susceptible pine species and many species of *Ribes*.

Bark beetles

Bark beetle outbreaks are occurring throughout the Rocky Mountain Region. All white pine species in the region are susceptible to bark beetles and limber pine appears to be a particularly suitable host for mountain pine beetle (Cerezeke 1995). The combined effects of WPBR and mountain pine beetle have caused extensive mortality in whitebark pine in the Northern and Intermountain Regions. Six and Adams (2006) found that under drought conditions, mountain pine beetles preferred severely infected whitebark pines. Similarly, Schwandt and Kegley (2004) found evidence suggesting that when mountain pine beetle populations were low (endemic), beetles were more likely to attack WPBR-infected whitebark pines.

The process of identifying and tending to plus trees represents a significant financial and ecological investment. Thus, it is imperative that plus trees are protected from bark beetle attack. The most effective method for protecting white pine plus trees from mountain pine beetle attack is to apply an appropriate, registered insecticide prior to beetle flight. Carbaryl has been highly effective in protecting whitebark pine plus trees from mountain pine beetle attacks in the Greater Yellowstone Area and would likely be as effective on other white pines in the Rocky Mountain Region. Permethrin and bifenthrin are also effective in protecting pines from mountain pine beetle attack.

Verbenone, a known anti-aggregation pheromone of mountain pine beetle, has been used to protect whitebark pines from mountain pine beetle attacks with moderate success in a study on the Lolo National Forest, Montana (Kegley and Gibson 2004). However, results in lodgepole and ponderosa pine stands have been inconsistent suggesting that results may vary among hosts (Amman and others 1991; Gibson and others 1991; Progar 2003). The efficacy of verbenone to protect limber, RM bristlecone, and southwestern white pine from mountain pine beetle attacks has not been evaluated. Although it is not as reliable and effective as carbaryl, verbenone may provide protection in circumstances where the use of insecticides is not an option. Efforts to test and improve verbenone effectiveness are underway in the Northern Region. Consultation with a Forest Health Specialist is strongly encouraged.

Seed Transfer Guidelines

The growth and health of planted trees is dependent on their local adaptation. As outlined by Mahalovich (2005), developing seed transfer guidelines is the first stage of an artificial regeneration strategy. Seed transfer rules are necessary to guide managers regarding how far away from a management unit seed can be collected and still be adapted to a planting location. Geneticists characterize patterns of variation, such as provenance (stand, population), family (trees from cones collected from one tree), individual, and sometimes clone, within a species for each trait. Seed transfer guidelines are based on how much variation is present at the provenance level. They emphasize consistent performance by limiting the consequences of any negative genotype by environment interactions (inconsistent performance across the landscape). These experiments, and the patterns of variation of the adaptive traits, provide insight into how a species is suited to its environment. Western white pine is considered to have a generalist adaptive strategy in the Northern Rockies (Rehfeldt 1979; Rehfeldt and Steinhoff 1970; Steinhoff 1979; Townsend and others 1972) whereas whitebark pine has a more intermediate adaptive strategy (Mahalovich and others 2006). Geographic patterns of genetic variation in adaptive traits in RM bristlecone pine are currently being studied, but little information is available on the distribution of adaptive traits of limber pine and southwestern white pine.

Whitebark pine in the Rocky Mountain Region is a member of the Greater Yellowstone-Grand Teton seed zone. There are no restrictions on elevation transfers, but seed from low (less than 49 percent) to moderate (50 to 70 percent) rust infection should not be planted on sites with high (greater than 70 percent) rust infection (Mahalovich and Dickerson 2004; Mahalovich and Hoff 2000). When planting in cold swales or frost pockets, seed sources that are both cold hardy and rust resistant should be selected (Mahalovich and others 2006).

Limber pine is currently separated into five seed zones (Great Basin, Southern Rockies, Northern Rockies, Columbia Plateau, and Nevada Humboldt); however, a region-wide common garden study has not been conducted. Similar to whitebark pine, seed from low to moderate rust infection should not be planted on sites with high rust infection. Seeds collected from phenotypically resistant trees in areas with high infection levels are suitable for planting on sites with low, moderate, or high infection levels. Lastly, seed should be moved no more than 700 ft (about 210 m) in elevation within a seed zone due to differences in pollen phenology and possible impacts on gene flow and diversity found among populations.

Established seed zones in the USDA Forest Service Seed Handbook FSH 2409.26f, Rocky Mountain Region should be followed for RM bristlecone and southwestern white pine. These seed zones are based on Cunningham's work (1975). Transfer of seed from low and moderate rust infection level stands to high infection level stands is prohibited (same as whitebark and limber pine). Seed zones for limber, bristlecone, and southwestern white pine can be revised as better information from genecology studies of adaptive traits becomes available. Maps of seed zones are included in appendix A.

Acknowledgments

This paper was supported by USDA Forest Service, Rocky Mountain Region, Forest Health Management. The authors are especially grateful for the thoughtful reviews and advice that Dave Conklin, John Guyon, Jim Hoffman, John Schwandt, and Jim Worrall provided on an earlier version of this manuscript. We also would like to thank Jim Blodgett, Brian Geils, Susan Gray, Erik Smith, Jeff Witcosky, and Gene Van Arsdel for their helpful comments. A special thanks to Brian Howell for preparing GIS maps. All photos were taken by the authors except figure 5, which was contributed by Isabelle Lebouce, Dorena Genetic Resource Center.

References

Amman, G.D.; Their, R.W.; Weatherby, J.C.; Rasmussen, L.A; Munson, A.S. 1991. Optimum dosage of verbenone to reduce infestation of mountain pine beetle in lodgepole pine stands of central Idaho. Res. Pap. INT-446. Ogden, UT: U.S. Department of Agriculture, Forest Service, Intermountain Forest and Range Experiment Station. 5 p.

Bailey, D.K. 1970. Phytogeography and taxonomy of *Pinus* subsection *Balfourianae*. Annals of the Missouri Botanical Garden. 57: 210-249.

Beam, R.D. 2005. [Personal communication]. Fort Collins, CO: Colorado State University, Department of Bioagricultural Sciences and Pest Management.

Berube, J.A. 1996. Use of tridemefon to control white pine blister rust. Forestry Chronicle. 72: 637-638.

Bingham, R.T. 1972. Taxonomy, crossability, and relative blister rust resistance of 5-needled white pines. p. 271-278. In: Bingham, R.T.; Hoff, R.J.; McDonald, G.I., eds. Biology of rust resistance in forest trees. Proc. NATO-IUFRO Advanced Study Institute. Moscow, ID: U.S. Department of Agriculture, Forest Service, Miscellaneous Publ. # 1221: 681 p.

Blodgett, J.T.; Sullivan, K.F. 2004a. First report of white pine blister rust on Rocky Mountain bristlecone pine. Plant Disease. 88: 311.

Blodgett, J.T.; Sullivan, K.F. 2004b. Letter to the superintendent of Great Sand Dunes National Park and Preserve. U.S. Department of Agriculture, Forest Service, Rocky Mountain Region, Renewable Resources. Service Trip Report RCSC-04-13. 2 p.

Brown, D.H. 1967. White pine blister rust survey in Montana and Wyoming 1966. U.S. Department of Agriculture, Forest Service, Northern Region, State and Private Forestry. Report 5270. 11 p.

Brown, D.H. 1978. Extension of the known distribution of *Cronartium ribicola* and *Arceuthobium cyanocarpum* on limber pine in Wyoming. Plant Disease Reporter. 62: 905.

Brown, D.H.; Graham, D.A. 1969. White pine blister rust survey in Wyoming, Idaho, and Utah: 1967. U.S. Department of Agriculture, Forest Service, Northern Region, State and Private Forestry. Report R3-94-2. 12 p.

Burns, K.S. 2006. White pine blister rust in the Sangre de Cristo and Wet Mountains of southern Colorado. U.S. Department of Agriculture, Forest Service, Rocky Mountain Region, Renewable Resources. Biological Evaluation R2-06-05. 22 p. Available: http://www.fs fed. us/r2/fhm/ [2006, March 21].

Burr, K.E.; Eramian, A.; Eggleston, K. 2001. Growing whitebark pine seedlings for restoration. In: Tomback, D.F.; Arno, S.F.; Keane, R.E., eds. 2001. Whitebark Pine Communities: Ecology and Restoration. Washington D.C.: Island Press: 325-345.

Carey, J.H. 1995. *Ribes lacustre*. In: Fire Effects Information System, [Online]. U.S. Department of Agriculture, Forest Service, Rocky Mountain Research Station, Fire Sciences Laboratory (Producer). Available: http://www. fs fed.us/database/feis/ [2006, February 28].

Cerezeke, H.F. 1995. Egg gallery, brood production, and adult characteristics of mountain pine beetle, *Dendroctonus ponderosae* Hopkins (Coleoptera: Scolytidae), in three pine hosts. Canadian Entomologist. 127: 955-965.

Charlton, J.W. 1963. Relating climate to eastern white pine blister rust infection hazard. Upper Darby, PA: U.S. Department of Agriculture, Forest Service, Eastern Region Report Library. 38 p.

Childs, T.W.; Kimmey, J.W. 1938. Studies on probable damage by blister rust in some representative stands of young western white pine. Journal of Agricultural Research. 57: 557-568.

Childs, T.W.; Bedwell, J.L.; Englerth, G.H. 1938. Blister rust infection on *Pinus albicaulis* in the northwest. Plant Disease Reporter. 22: 139-140.

Conklin, D.A. 2004. Development of the white pine blister rust outbreak in New Mexico. U.S. Department of Agriculture, Forest Service, Southwestern Region, Forestry and Forest Health. Biological Evaluation R3-04-01. 15 p.

Conklin, D.A. 2006. [Personal communication]. Albuquerque, NM: U.S. Department of Agriculture, Forest Service, Southwest Region.

Crump, A.V.; Jacobi, W.R.; Burns, K.S.; Howell, B.E. [In preparation]. Fort Collins, CO: Colorado State University, Department of Bioagricultural Sciences and Pest Management.

Cunningham, R.A. 1975. Provisional tree and shrub seed zones for the Great Plains. Res. Pap. RM-150. Fort Collins, CO: U.S. Department of Agriculture, Forest Service, Rocky Mountain Forest and Range Experiment Station. 15 p.

Daly, C.; Gibson, W.P.; Taylor, G.H.; Johnson, G.L.; Pasteris, P. 2002. A knowledge-based approach to the statistical mapping of climate. Climate Research. 22: 99-113.

Draper, M.A.; Walla, J.A. 1993. First report of *Cronartium ribicola* in North Dakota. Plant Disease. 77: 952.

Ehrlich, J.; Opie, R.S. 1940. Mycelial extent beyond blister rust cankers on *Pinus monticola*. Phytopathology. 30(7): 611-620.

Geils, B.W. 2006. [Personal communication]. Flagstaff, AZ: U.S. Department of Agriculture, Forest Service, Rocky Mountain Research Station.

Geils, B.W.; Conklin, D.A.; Van Arsdel, E.P. 1999. A preliminary hazard model of white pine blister rust for the Sacramento Ranger District, Lincoln National Forest. Res. Note RMRS-RN-6. Fort Collins, CO: U.S. Department of Agriculture, Forest Service, Rocky Mountain Research Station. 6 p.

Gibson, K.E.; Schmitz, R.F.; Amman, G.D.; Oakes, R.D. 1991. Mountain pine beetle response to different verbenone dosages in pine stands of western Montana. Res. Pap. INT-444. Ogden, UT: U.S. Department of Agriculture, Forest Service, Intermountain Forest and Range Experiment Station. 11 p.

Greater Yellowstone Whitebark Pine Monitoring Working Group. 2006. Monitoring whitebark in the Greater Yellowstone Ecosystem, 2005 Annual Report. p. 73-80, In: Schwartz, C.C.; Haroldson, M.A.; West, K., eds. Yellowstone grizzly bear investigations: annual report of the Interagency Grizzly Bear Study Team, 2005. U.S. Geological Survey, Bozeman, MT.

Hagle, S.K.; Grasham, J. 1988. Biological and economic feasibility of pruning and excising western white pines for blister rust control. Missoula, MT: U.S. Department of Agriculture, Forest Service, Cooperative Forestry and Pest Management. Rep. 88-6. 14 p.

Hagle, S.K.; McDonald, G.I.; Norby, E.A. 1989. White pine blister rust in northern Idaho and western Montana: Alternatives for integrated management. Gen. Tech. Rep. INT-261. Ogden, UT: U.S. Department of Agriculture, Forest Service, Intermountain Research Station. 35 p.

Hawksworth, F.G. 1990. White pine blister rust in southern New Mexico. Plant Disease. 74: 938.

Hoff, R.J.; Bingham, R.T.; McDonald, G.I. 1980. Relative blister rust resistance of white pines. European Journal of Forest Pathology. 10: 307-316.

Hoff, R.J.; Ferguson, D.E.; McDonald, G.I.; Keane, R.E. 2001. Strategies for managing whitebark pine in the presence of white pine blister rust. In: Tomback, D.F.; Arno, S.F.; Keane, R.E, eds. 2001. Whitebark Pine Communities: Ecology and Restoration. Washington, DC: Island Press: 346-366.

Hoff, R.J.; McDonald, G.I.; Bingham, R.T. 1976. Mass selection for blister rust resistance: A method for natural regeneration of western white pine. Research Note INT-202. Ogden, UT: U.S. Department of Agriculture, Forest Service, Intermountain Forest and Range Experiment Station. 11 p.

Hoffman, J.T. 2006. [Personal communication]. Boise, ID: U.S. Department of Agriculture, Forest Service, Intermountain Region.

Howard, J.L. 2002. *Pinus albicaulis*. In: Fire Effects Information System, [Online]. U.S. Department of Agriculture, Forest Service, Rocky Mountain Research Station, Fire Sciences Laboratory (Producer). Available: http://www.fs fed.us/database/feis/ [2006, February 28].

Howard, J.L. 2004. *Pinus aristata*. In: Fire Effects Information System, [Online]. U.S. Department of Agriculture, Forest Service, Rocky Mountain Research Station, Fire Sciences Laboratory (Producer). Available: www.fs fed.us/database/feis [2006, February 28].

Howell, B.E.; Burns, K.S.; Kearns, H.S.J. 2006. Biological evaluation of a model for predicting presence of white pine blister rust in Colorado based on climatic variables and susceptible white pine species distribution. U.S. Department of Agriculture, Forest Service, Rocky Mountain Region, Renewable Resources. Biological Evaluation. R2-06-04. 15 p. Available: http://www. fs fed.us/r2/fhm/ [2006, March 21].

Hungerford, R.D.; Williams, R.E.; Marsden, M.A. 1982. Thinning and pruning western white pine: a potential for reducing mortality due to blister rust. Res. Note INT-322. Ogden, UT: U.S. Department of Agriculture, Forest Service, Intermountain Forest and Range Experiment Station. 7 p.

Hunt, R.S. 1982. White pine blister rust control in British Columbia I. The possibilities of control by branch removal. The Forestry Chronicle. 59: 136-138.

Hunt, R.S. 1983. White pine blister rust in British Columbia II. Can stands be hazard rated? The Forestry Chronicle. 59: 30-33.

Johnson, D.R.; Kinloch, B.B., Jr.; McCain, A.H. 1992. Triadimefon controls white pine blister rust on sugar pine in a greenhouse test. Tree Planters Notes. 43: 7-10.

Johnson, D.W.; Jacobi, W.R. 2000. First report of white pine blister rust in Colorado. Plant Disease. 84: 595.

Johnson, K.A. 2001. *Pinus flexilis*. In: Fire Effects Information System, [Online]. U.S. Department of Agriculture, Forest Service, Rocky Mountain Research Station, Fire Sciences Laboratory (Producer). Available: http://www.fs fed.us/database/feis/ [2006, February 28].

Katovich, S.A.; O'Brien, J.G.; Mielke, M.E.; Ostry, M.E. 2004. Restoration and management of eastern white pine within high blister rust hazard zones in the Lakes States. In: Shepperd, W.D.; Eskew, L.G., eds. Silviculture in special places: Proceedings of the 2003 National Silviculture Workshop, RMRS-P-34. Fort Collins, CO: U.S. Department of Agriculture, Forest Service, Rocky Mountain Research Station: 135-145. Available: http://www fs.fed.us/rm/pubs/rmrs_p034/ rmrs_p034_146_155.pdf [2007, Sept. 5].

Kearns, H.S.J. 2005. White pine blister rust in the central Rocky Mountains: Modeling current status and potential impacts. Fort Collins, CO: Colorado State University. 243 p. Dissertation.

Kearns, H.S.J.; Burns, K.S. 2005. Distribution, incidence, and severity of white pine blister rust on the Medicine Bow National Forest. U.S. Department of Agriculture, Forest Service, Rocky Mountain Region, Renewable Resources. Biological Evaluation. R2-06-01. 18 p. Available: http://www.fs.fed.us/r2/fhm/ [2006, March 21].

Kearns, H.S.J.; Jacobi, W.R. 2007. The distribution and incidence of white pine blister rust in central and southeastern Wyoming and northern Colorado. Can. J. For. Res. 37: 462-472.

Kegley, S.; Gibson, K. 2004. Protecting whitebark pine trees from mountain pine beetle attack using verbenone. Missoula, MT: U.S. Department of Agriculture, Forest Service, Northern Region, Forest Health Protection. Report 04-8. 4 p.

Kendall, K.C.; Keane, R.E. 2001. Whitebark pine decline: Infection, mortality, and population trends. In: Tomback, D.F.; Arno, S.F.; Keane, R.E., eds. Whitebark Pine Communities. Washington, DC: Island Press: 221-242.

Kinloch, Jr., B.B.; Dupper, G.E. 1999. Evidence of cytoplasmic inheritance of virulence in *Cronartium ribicola* to major gene resistance in sugar pine. Phytopathology. 89: 192-196.

Klutsh, J.G. 2005. [Personal communication]. Fort Collins, CO: Colorado State University, Department of Bioagricultural Sciences and Pest Management.

Krebill, R.G. 1964. Blister rust found on limber pine in northern Wasatch Mountains. Plant Disease Reporter. 50: 532.

Lehrer, G.F. 1982. Pathological pruning: a useful tool in white pine blister rust control. Plant Disease. 66(12): 1138-1139.

Lundquist, J.E.; Geils, B.W.; Johnson, D.W. 1992. White pine blister rust on limber pine in South Dakota. Plant Disease. 76: 538.

Mahalovich, M.F. 2000. Whitebark pine restoration strategy—some genetic considerations. Nutcracker Notes. 11: 6-9.

Mahalovich, M.F. 2005. Seed transfer rules and expert systems. Skills for Tree Improvement Personnel Workshop, April 5-7, Coeur d'Alene, ID, U.S. Department of Agriculture, Forest Service, Northern Region: 8 p.

Mahalovich, M.F. [In preparation]. FSH 2409.26f Seed Handbook. Golden, CO: U.S. Department of Agriculture, Forest Service, Rocky Mountain Region.

Mahalovich, M.F.; Burr, K.E.; Foushee, D.L. 2006. Whitebark pine germination, rust resistance and cold hardiness among seed sources in the Inland Northwest: Planting strategies for restoration. In: National proceedings: Forest and Conservation Nursery Association; 2005 July 18-20; Park City, UT, USA. Proc. RMRS-P-43. Fort Collins, CO: U.S. Department of Agriculture, Forest Service, Rocky Mountain Research Station: 91-101.

Mahalovich, M.F.; Dickerson, G.A. 2004. Whitebark pine genetic restoration program for the Intermountain West (United States). In: Sniezko, R.A.; Samman, S.; Schlarbaum, S.E.; Kriebel, H.B., eds. 2004. Breeding and genetic resources of five-needle pines: growth, adaptability and pest resistance; 2001 July 23–27; Medford, OR, USA. IUFRO Working Party 2.02.15. Proc. RMRS-P-32. Fort Collins, CO: U.S. Department of Agriculture, Forest Service, Rocky Mountain Research Station: 181-187.

Mahalovich, M.F.; Hoff, R.J. 2000. Whitebark pine operational cone collection instructions and seed transfer guidelines. Nutcracker Notes. 11: 10-13.

Marshall, K.A. 1995a. *Ribes cereum*. In: Fire Effects Information System, [Online]. U.S. Department of Agriculture, Forest Service, Rocky Mountain Research Station, Fire Sciences Laboratory (Producer). Available: http://www.fs fed.us/database/feis/ [2006, February 28].

Marshall, K.A. 1995b. *Ribes montigenum*. In: Fire Effects Information System, [Online]. U.S. Department of Agriculture, Forest Service, Rocky Mountain Research Station, Fire Sciences Laboratory (Producer). Available: http://www.fs fed.us/database/feis/ [2006, February 28].

Martin, J.F. 1944. *Ribes* eradication effectively controls white pine blister rust. Journal of Forestry. 42: 255-260.

McDonald, G.I.; Hoff, R.J. 2001. Blister rust: an introduced plague. In: Tomback, D.F.; Arno, S.F.; Keane, R.E., eds. 2001. Whitebark Pine Communities: Ecology and Restoration. Washington, DC: Island Press: 193-220.

McDonald, G.I.; Richardson, B.A.; Zambino, P.J.; Klopfenstein, N.B.; Kim, M.-S. 2006. *Pedicularis* and *Castilleja* are natural hosts of *Cronartium ribicola* in North America: a first report. Forest Pathology. 36: 73-82.

McKinney, S.T.; Tomback, D.F. 2007. The influence of white pine blister rust on seed dispersal in whitebark pine. Canadian Journal of Forest Research. 37: 1044-1057.

Newcomb, M. 2003. White pine blister rust, whitebark pine, and *Ribes* species in the Greater Yellowstone Area. Missoula, MT: University of Montana. 66 p. Thesis.

Offord, H.R.; Quick, C.R.; Moss, V.D. 1958. Blister rust control aided by the use of chemicals for killing *Ribes*. Journal of Forestry. 56: 12-18.

Ostrofsky, W.D.; Rumpf, T.; Struble, D.; Bradbury, R. 1988. Incidence of white pine blister rust in Maine after 70 years of a *Ribes* eradication program. Plant Disease. 72: 967-970.

Pavek, D.S. 1993. *Pinus strobiformis*. In: Fire Effects Information System, [Online]. U.S. Department of Agriculture, Forest Service, Rocky Mountain Research Station, Fire Sciences Laboratory (Producer). Available: http://www.fs fed.us/database/feis/ [2006, February 28].

Price, R.A.; Liston, A.; Strauss, S.H. 1998. Phylogeny and systematics of *Pinus*. In: Richardson, D.M., ed. Ecology and Biogeography of *Pinus*. Cape Town, South Africa: Cambridge University Press: 49-68.

Progar, R.A. 2003. Verbenone reduces mountain pine beetle attack in lodgepole pine. Western Journal of Applied Forestry. 18(4): 229-232.

Rehfeldt, G.E. 1979. Ecotypic differentiation in populations of *Pinus monticola* in North Idaho—myth or reality? The American Naturalist. 114(5): 627-636.

Rehfeldt, G.E.; Steinhoff, R.J. 1970. Height growth in western white pine progenies. Res. Note INT-123. Ogden, UT: U.S. Department of Agriculture, Forest Service, Intermountain Forest and Range Experiment Station. 4 p.

Samman, S.; Schwandt, J.W.; Wilson, J.L. 2003. Managing for healthy white pine ecosystems in the United States to reduce the impacts of white pine blister rust. U.S. Department of Agriculture, Forest Service, Northern Region. Report R1-03-118. 10 p.

Schnepf, C.C.; Schwandt, J.W. 2006. Pruning western white pine: a vital tool for species restoration. Pacific Northwest Extension Publication 584. 63 p.

Schoettle, A.W. 2004a. Ecological roles of five-needle pine in Colorado: potential consequences of their loss. In: Sniezko, R.; Samman, S.; Schlarbaum, S.; Kriebel, H., eds. Breeding and genetic resources of five-needle pines: growth adaptability and pest resistance. 2001 July 24-25; Medford, OR. IUFRO Working Party 2.02.15. Proc. RMRS-P-32. Ogden, UT: U.S. Department of Agriculture, Forest Service, Rocky Mountain Research Station: 124-135.

Schoettle, A.W. 2004b. Developing proactive management options to sustain bristlecone and limber pine ecosystems in the presence of a non-native pathogen. In: Shepperd, W.D.; Eskew, L.G., eds. Silviculture in special places: proceedings of the 2003 National Silviculture Workshop, RMRS-P-34. Fort Collins, CO: U.S. Department of Agriculture, Forest Service, Rocky Mountain Research Station: 146-155. Available: http://www fs fed.us/rm/pubs/rmrs_p034/rmrs_p034_146_155.pdf [2007, Sept. 5].

Schoettle, A.W.; Berger, C.A.; Bonnet, V.H. 2003. Proactive conservation options for bristlecone pine forests in the presence of an exotic pathogen—use of fire? In: Abstracts—The Ecological Society of America 88th annual meeting, August 3-8, 2003, Savannah, GA. The Ecological Society of America, Washington, DC. 301 p.

Schoettle, A.W.; Rochelle, S.G. 2000. Morphological variation of *Pinus flexilis* (Pinaceae), a bird-dispersed pine, across a range of elevations. American Journal of Botany. 87: 1797-1806.

Schoettle, A.W.; Sniezko, R.A. 2007. Proactive intervention to sustain high elevation pine ecosystems threatened by white pine blister rust. Journal of Forest Research. 12: 327-336.

Schwandt, J.W. 2006. Whitebark pine in peril: a case for restoration. U.S. Department of Agriculture, Forest Service, Northern Region, Forest Health Protection. Report R1-06-28. 20 p. Available: http://www fs.fed.us/r1-r4/spf/fhp/whitebark_pine/WBPCover_3.htm [2007, March 9].

Schwandt, J.; Kegley, S. 2004. Mountain pine beetle, blister rust, and their interaction on whitebark pine at Trout Lake and Fisher Peak in northern Idaho from 2001-2003. U.S. Department of Agriculture, Forest Service, Intermountain Region, Forest Health Protection. Report 04-9. 6 p.

Schwandt, J.W.; Marsden, M.A.; McDonald, G.I. 1994. Pruning and thinning effects on white pine survival and volume in northern Idaho. In: Proceedings of the Symposium on interior cedar-hemlock-white pine forests: ecology and management. March 2-4, 1993. Spokane, Washington. Department of Natural Resource Sciences, Washington State University, Pullman, WA, 99164-6410: 167-172.

Six, D.L.; Adams, J. 2006. White pine blister rust seerity and selection of individual whitebark pine by the mountain pine beetle (Coleoptera: Curculionidae, Scolytinae). J. Entomol. Sci. 42(3): 345-353.

Smith, J.P.; Hoffman, J.T.; Sullivan, K.F.; Van Arsdel, E.P.; Vogler, D.R. 2000. First report of white pine blister rust in Nevada. Plant Disease. 84: 594.

Steinhoff, R.J. 1979. Variation in early growth of western white pine in northern Idaho. Res. Pap. INT-222. Ogden, UT: U.S. Department of Agriculture, Forest Service, Intermountain Forest and Range Experiment Station. 22 p.

Stillinger, C.R. 1947. Pruning white pine reproduction to salvage a stand heavily infested with white pine blister rust. Serial 138. Washington, DC: U.S. Department of Agriculture, Bureau of Entomology and Plant Quarantine. 21 p.

Tomback, D.F.; Clary, J.K.; Koehler, J.; Hoff, R.J.; Arno, S.F. 1995. The effects of blister rust on post-fire regeneration of whitebark pine: the Sundance burn of northern Idaho (USA). Conservation Biology. 9: 654-664.

Tomback, D.F.; Keane, R.E.; McCaughey, W.W.; Smith, C. 2004. Methods for surveying and monitoring whitebark pine for blister rust infection and damage. Whitebark Pine Ecosystem Foundation, Missoula, MT. 28 p.

Tomback, D.F.; Kendell, K.C. 2001. Biodiversity losses: the downward spiral. In: Tomback, D.F.; Arno, S.F.; Keane, R.E., eds. Whitebark Pine Communities. Washington, DC: Island Press: 243-262.

Townsend, A.M.; Hanover, J.W.; Barnes, B.V. 1972. Altitudinal variation in photosynthesis, growth, and monoterpene composition of western white pine (*Pinus monticola* Dougl.) seedlings. Silvae Genetica. 21: 133-139.

U.S. Department of Agriculture Forest Service. 1950. Central Rocky Mountain Region Routine Travel Routes and Important Forest Units Scouting 1950. On file with W.R. Jacobi, Colorado State University, Fort Collins, CO.

U.S. Department of Agriculture Forest Service. 1951. Central Rocky Mountain Region Routine Travel Routes and Important Forest Units Scouting 1951. On file with W.R. Jacobi, Colorado State University, Fort Collins, CO.

U.S. Department of Agriculture Forest Service. 1959. Central Rocky Mountain Region Routine Travel Routes and Important Forest Units Scouting 1959. On file with W.R. Jacobi, Colorado State University, Fort Collins, CO.

Van Arsdel, E.P.; Geils, B.W. 2004. The *Ribes* of Colorado and New Mexico and their rust fungi. FHTET-04-13. Fort Collins, CO: U.S. Department of Agriculture, Forest Service, Rocky Mountain Research Station. 32 p.

Van Arsdel, E.P.; Geils, B.W.; Zambino, P.J. 2005. Epidemiology for hazard rating of white pine blister rust. In: Guyon, J., comp. Proceedings of the 53rd Western International Forest Disease Work Conference; 2005 August 26-29; Jackson, WY. Ogden, UT: U.S. Department of Agriculture, Forest Service, Intermountain Region: 49-62.

Van Arsdel, E.P. 1961. Growing white pines in the Lake States to avoid blister rust. Paper No 92. St. Paul, MN: U.S. Department of Agriculture, Forest Service, Lake States Forest Experiment Station. 11 p.

Vogler, D.R. 2005. [Personal communication]. Placerville, CA: U.S. Department of Agriculture, Forest Service, Pacific Southwest Region, Institute of Forest Genetics.

Vogler, D.R.; Charlet, D.A. 2004. First report of the white pine blister rust fungus (*Cronartium ribicola*) infecting whitebark pine (*Pinus albicaulis*) and *Ribes* spp. in the Jarbidge Mountains of northeastern Nevada. Plant Disease. 88: 772.

Vogler, D.; Delfino-Mix, A.; Schoettle, A.W. 2006. White pine blister rust in high elevation white pines: Screening for simply inherited hypersensitive resistance. In: Guyon, J., comp. Proceedings of the 53rd Western International Forest Disease Work Conference; 2005 August 26-29; Jackson, WY. Ogden, UT: U.S. Department of Agriculture, Forest Service, Intermountain Region: 73-82.

Zambino, P.J.; Richardson, B.A.; McDonald, G.I. 2007. First Report of the white pine blister rust fungus, *Cronartium ribicola*, on *Pedicularis bracteosa*. Plant Disease. 91: 467.

Appendix A—Seed zone maps

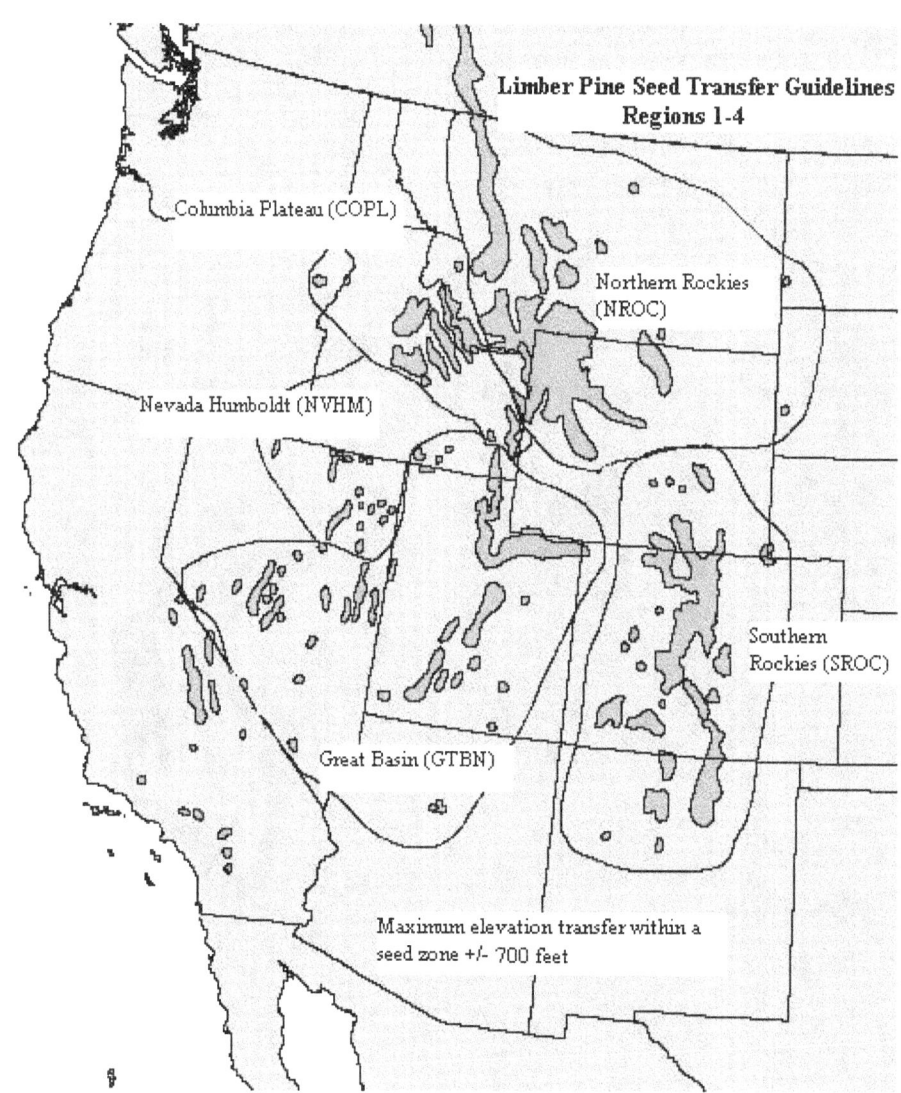

Figure A1—Limber pine seed zones.

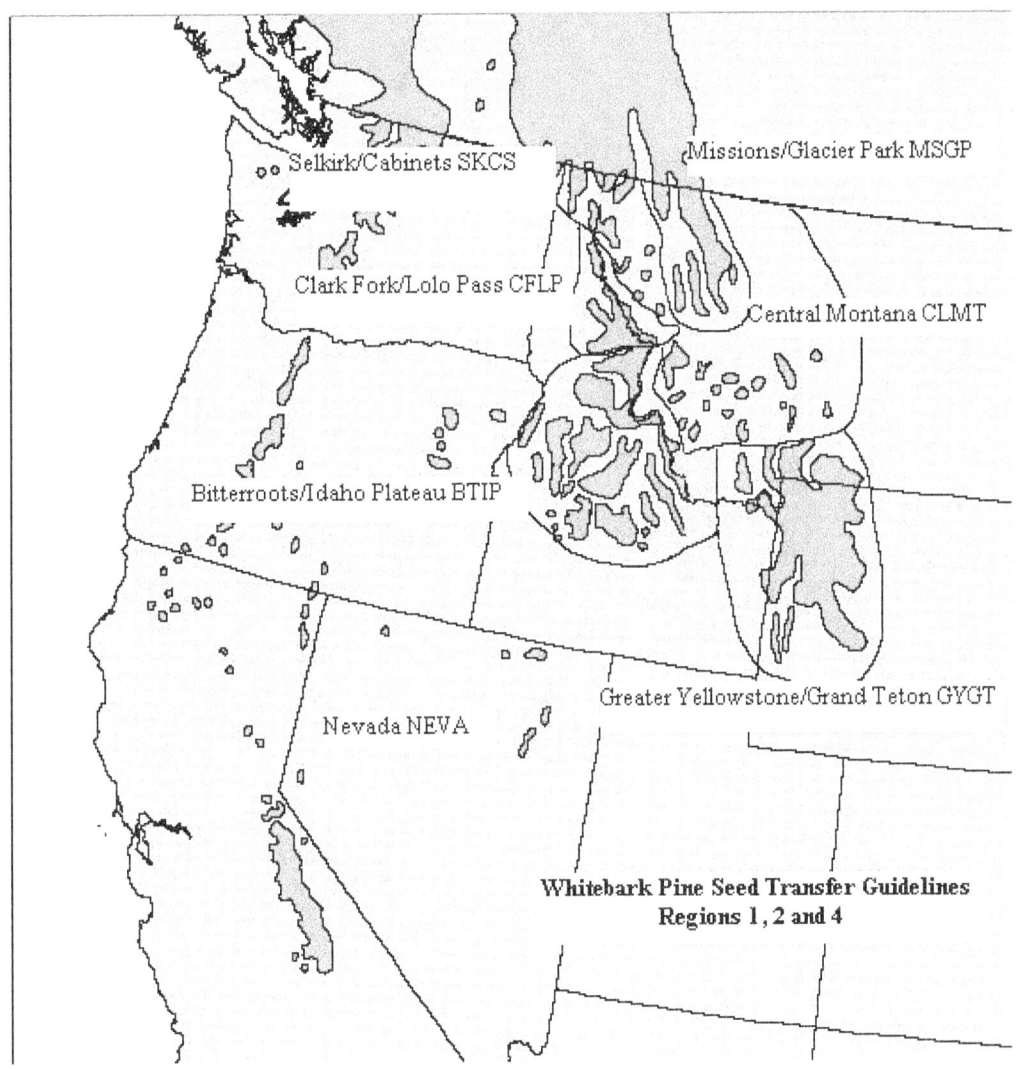

Figure A2—Whitebark pine seed zones.

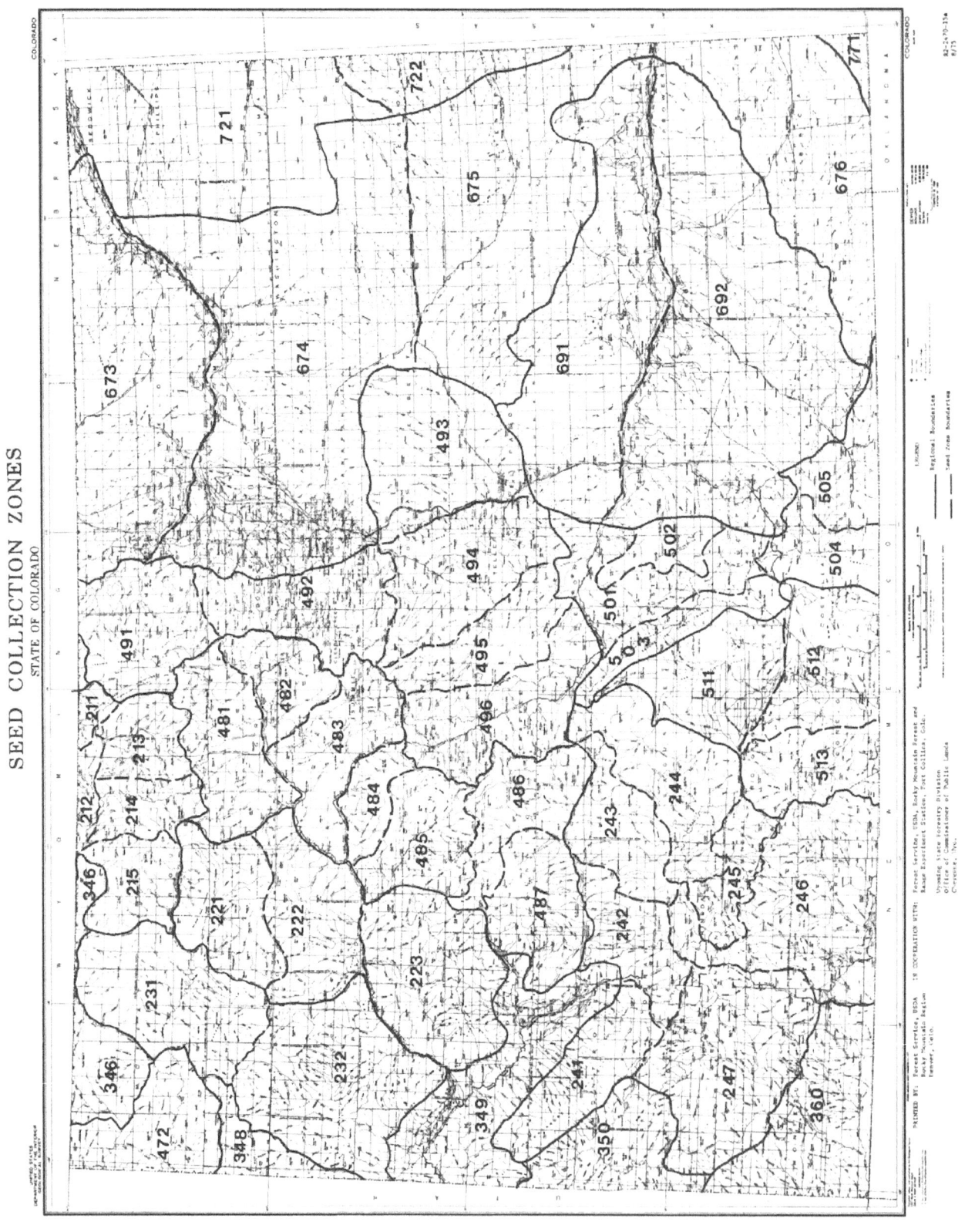

Figure A3—Established seed collection zones in Colorado.

SEED COLLECTION ZONES

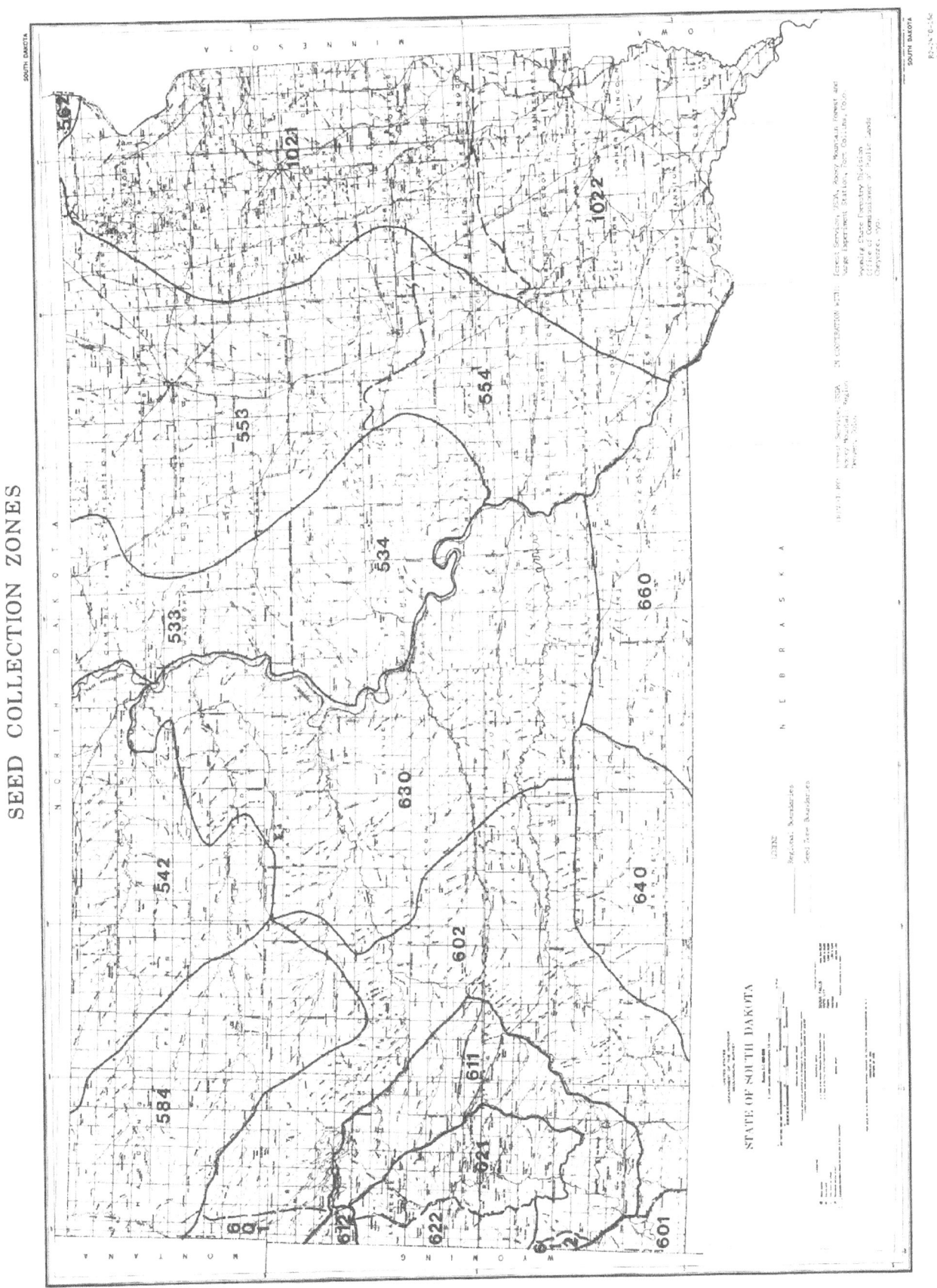

Figure A4—Established seed collection zones in South Dakota.

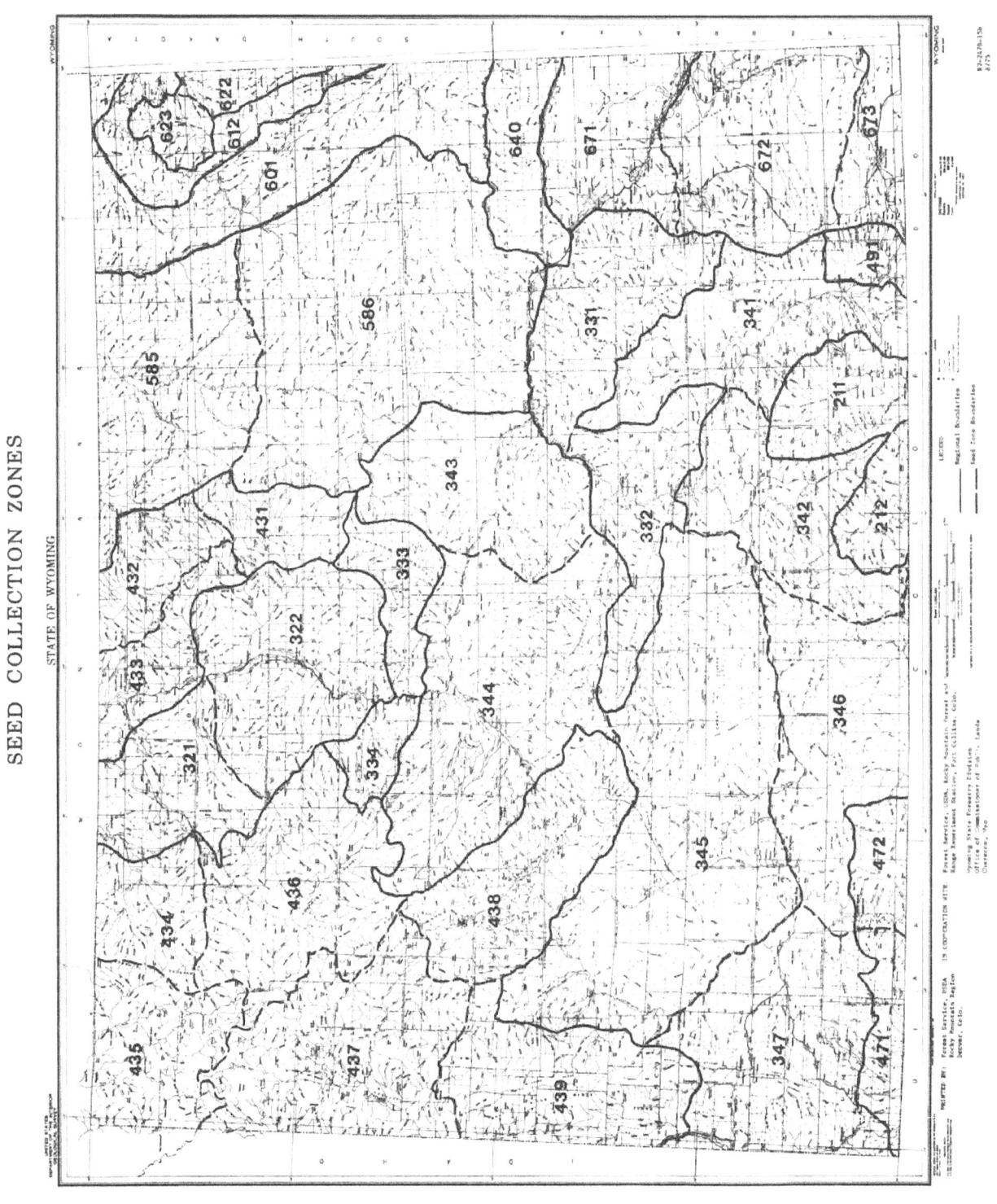

Figure A5—Established seed collection zones in Wyoming.

USDA Forest Service RMRS-GTR-206. 2008.

Publishing Services Staff

Managing Editor · Lane Eskew

Page Composition & Printing · Nancy Chadwick

Editorial Assistant · Loa Collins

Contract Editor · Kristi Coughlon

Page Composition & Printing · Connie Lemos

Distribution · Richard Schneider

Online Publications & Graphics · Suzy Stephens

RMRS
ROCKY MOUNTAIN RESEARCH STATION

The Rocky Mountain Research Station develops scientific information and technology to improve management, protection, and use of the forests and rangelands. Research is designed to meet the needs of the National Forest managers, Federal and State agencies, public and private organizations, academic institutions, industry, and individuals. Studies accelerate solutions to problems involving ecosystems, range, forests, water, recreation, fire, resource inventory, land reclamation, community sustainability, forest engineering technology, multiple use economics, wildlife and fish habitat, and forest insects and diseases. Studies are conducted cooperatively, and applications may be found worldwide.

Research Locations

Flagstaff, Arizona	Reno, Nevada
Fort Collins, Colorado*	Albuquerque, New Mexico
Boise, Idaho	Rapid City, South Dakota
Moscow, Idaho	Logan, Utah
Bozeman, Montana	Ogden, Utah
Missoula, Montana	Provo, Utah

*Station Headquarters, Natural Resources Research Center, 2150 Centre Avenue, Building A, Fort Collins, CO 80526.

www.ingramcontent.com/pod-product-compliance
Lightning Source LLC
Chambersburg PA
CBHW082203290526
45794CB00008B/3409